7 STEPS
$CHOLARSHIP $UCCE$$

start in Middle School

TIPS for Teens who want a great ACT & SAT score plus scholarships galore.

by SHAUN LORRAINE BROWN

mother of 5 prolific scholarship winners

Copyright © 2015 by Shaun Lorraine Brown
Cover and Internal Design © 2015 by Brown's Red Barn

All rights reserved. No part of this book may be reproduced in any form or by any electronic or mechanical means including information storage and retrieval systems — except in the case of brief quotations embodied in critical articles or reviews — without written permission from the publisher.

ISBN-13: 978-0692400937

Printed by CreateSpace, an Amazon.com Company
Available from Amazon.com and other outlets
Available on Kindle and other devices

All brand names and product names used in this book are trademarks, registered trademarks, or trade names of their respective holders. CreateSpace is not associated with any product or vendor in this book.

Brown, Shaun Lorraine, author.

Seven Steps to Scholarship Success start in Middle School; Tips for Teens who want a great ACT and SAT score plus scholarships galore.

IF YOU ARE A STUDENT IN MIDDLE SCHOOL OR HIGH SCHOOL, THIS BOOK IS FOR YOU.

PARENTS ARE WELCOME TO LOOK, AND WILL FIND A FEW 'PARENT' TIPS AT THE BACK. BUT THIS BOOK IS PRIMARILY FOR THE STUDENT WHO WANTS TO CREATE THEIR OWN SUCCESS WITH GRADES, STANDARDIZED TESTS, COLLEGE ADMISSIONS AND SCHOLARSHIPS.

Thank you to my children —Kyle, Kendra, Drew, Stephanie, and Trevor— who helped me obtain the knowledge to provide these steps and strategies for you.

And thank you to my husband Nathan Brown for making it possible for me to tackle this project.

CONTENTS

CHAPTER 1
FOR FRESHMEN
THE GOAL — 1

CHAPTER 2
FOR FRESHMEN (AND 8TH GRADERS)
THE GRADES — 5
- Get a planner — 8
- Talk to your teachers — 8
- Early bird gets the grades — 9
- Extra credit — 10
- Study sessions — 11
- Eyes on the prize — 12
  - Amazing Grades Checklist — 13

CHAPTER 3
FOR FRESHMEN (AND 8TH GRADERS)
THE CLASSES — 15
- Know the required classes — 15
- Take advanced classes — 17

CHAPTER 4
FOR FRESHMEN
THE LISTS — 23
- Volunteer community service — 24
- Honors, awards & achievements — 28
  - Try new things — 29
  - Ask your teachers — 31
  - Search the internet — 31
- Leadership experience — 32
- Activities & interests — 34
- Work experience — 36
- One more list - STEM activities — 38

CHAPTER 5
FOR SOPHOMORES

THE TESTS — 45
Take the test early — 49
Take the test twice — 53
Know the test — 56
Know what parts are required — 56
Know the content — 57
Know the structure and format — 59
To guess or not? — 62
Guessing on the SAT — 63
Guessing on the ACT — 64
The good guess — 64
Standardized Test Prep Checklist — 67

CHAPTER 6
FOR JUNIORS & SENIORS

THE SCHOLARSHIPS — 69
Finding scholarships — 70
Your school counselor — 70
Community resources — 71
Upper class-men — 74
Online searches — 75
The applications — 77
Deadlines — 78
Transcripts — 79
Class rank — 79
Letters of recommendation — 80
Save, Save, Save and REUSE! — 80
Scholarship Application Checklist — 81

CHAPTER 7
FOR SENIORS

THE PAYOFF — 83
Be grateful — 84

APPENDIX
FOR PARENTS

Clear the path — 92

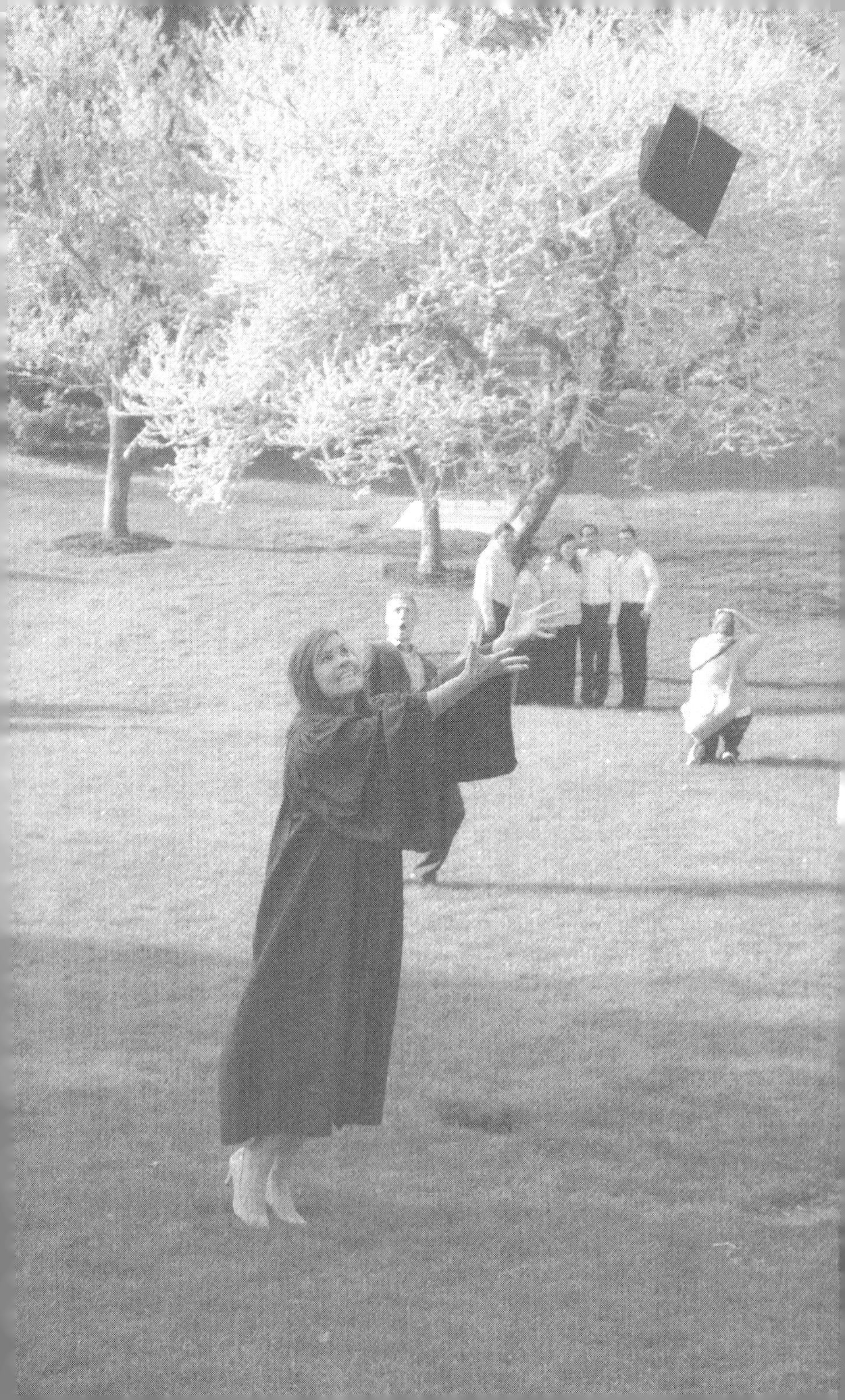

CHAPTER 1

FOR FRESHMEN

THE GOAL

Imagine the celebration on your high school graduation day if you toss your hat in the air, knowing you are accepted to the college you want to attend and you have scholarships to pay for it! Dreaming of such a celebration is the first step to making it happen, but the next few steps are captured in the chapters of this little book. To begin with, you need to turn this dream into a goal you are willing to work for.

THE GOAL: GET ACCEPTED TO THE COLLEGE OF MY CHOICE & GET SCHOLARSHIPS TO PAY FOR MY EDUCATION.

And as you have probably heard before, writing something down is what makes it a goal.

So insert the college (or colleges) of your choice, and make this your goal. Write it down everywhere; in your journal, on the top of your math notebook, on the sidewalk (with chalk), on a piece of paper you hang above your bed, or perhaps right here in this little book.

The dream can become a reality, and the steps are not complex. They are not even overly difficult or time consuming. Your path to achieving this dream hinges on your willingness to get started now, and to do the simple things that add up to success.

So put down the remote, or the cell phone or the game controller. Write down your goal and read on to find out how you can make this goal a reality.

MY GOAL: _____
_____
_____

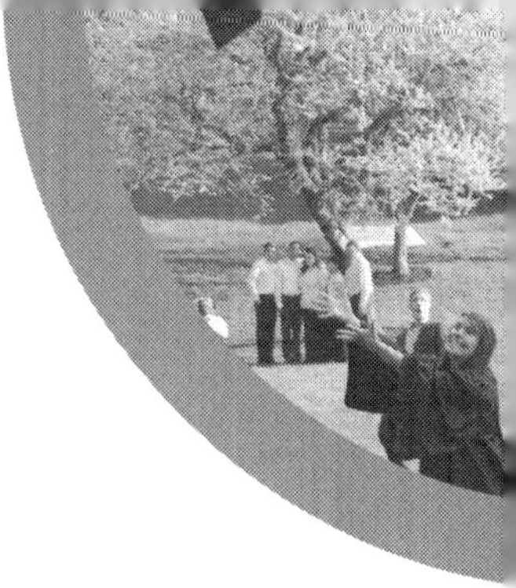

4   SCHOLARSHIP SUCCESS

CHAPTER 2
FOR FRESHMEN (AND 8TH GRADERS)

THE GRADES

We have always told our students,

> "GETTING INTO COLLEGE IS YOUR JOB RIGHT NOW. PUT IN THE TIME AND IT WILL PAY OFF IN SCHOLARSHIPS."

And it has paid off. Of our five kids, every single one has been accepted to the school of their choice. And all have received scholarships to cover the cost of their tuition. In several cases, the kids have covered their books, housing, and food expenses as well through scholarships. None of our children have student loans (except the occasional $100 or so from Dad when food funds run short at the end of semester). Our oldest daughter has graduated with no student loan debt and the other four are on track to do the same.

Grades play a big part in your ability to achieve your goals. Your college application is probably your most important scholarship application you will complete, because many schools give scholarships based on your initial application. You need to know that research shows most colleges consider grades first and foremost above any other information about you. A 2011 study conducted by the National Association for College Admissions Counseling (NACAC), indicated that 84.3% of colleges participating in the 2011 survey looked at grades first.[1]

THE FIRST AND MOST IMPORTANT USE OF YOUR TIME IS GETTING GOOD GRADES.

Sometimes you take classes with teachers you do not like, or subjects that you do not find interesting, but none of that will matter to the college admissions official who will look at your grades and your test scores before

---

[1] National Association for College Admission Counseling. (2011) *Admission Trends Survey*.retrieved from http://www.nacacnet.org/studentinfo/articles/Pages/Factors-in-the-Admission-Decision.aspx

deciding if you will get invited to come to their university. And good grades always help on scholarship applications, even when the criteria for a scholarship is partially need based.

No matter what the challenge, get good grades. High school in the United States is not too hard for any motivated, committed student. In 2014 here are the grade point averages of incoming freshmen for some universities in the United States: [2]

2014	GPA of incoming Freshmen
Harvard	3.94 - average GPA of those admitted
Florida State University	3.8 to 4.0 - average GPA of middle 50% admitted
Stanford	95% admitted had a GPA above 3.70. 73% had a 4.0
Brigham Young University	3.8 - average GPA of those admitted
U of California Berkeley	3.89 - average unweighted GPA of those admitted

---

[2] http://features.thecrimson.com/2013/frosh-survey/admissions.html
http://admissions.fsu.edu/freshman/admissions/requirements.cfm
http://admission.stanford.edu/basics/selection/profile.html
http://yfacts.byu.edu/Article?id=143
http://admissions.berkeley.edu/studentprofile

Let the desire to have someone else pay for your college experience motivate you to put in the time and effort necessary for good grades. There are no tricks to getting good grades, but here are a few tips to help you in your quest.

GET A PLANNER

Write down assignment due dates, quiz dates, test dates, and end of semester projects. This will help you avoid having multiple deadlines that surprise you late in the game. Once you've written everything down, you can decide when you need to tackle certain projects and where you can fit in study time.

TALK TO YOUR TEACHERS

If you get to know your teachers and share your goals with them, they will be more likely to support you and help you identify ways to be successful in their class. Most teachers have great respect for a motivated student, and will become your advocate, giving you guidance to help you succeed and making you aware if your grade happens to slip.

My middle son carried a 4.0 all through high school. As a senior, he discovered his responsibilities as Student Body President gobbled up a lot of time. When his grades started to dip in one or two classes, his teachers regularly notified him of the slip so he could do what was necessary to keep his 4.0 GPA.

EARLY BIRD GETS THE GRADES

Pay attention to your grades early in the semester. If your teachers don't regularly give you a progress report, then ask. When you know where you stand, you can determine if extra work or study is necessary.

And don't forget in some school districts, certain classes from your eighth grade year can become part of your high school GPA. If you take Algebra as an eighth grader, many schools place that class on your high school transcript. Sometimes they let you choose if you want the grade on your high school transcript, but sometimes they don't. So don't mess around in eighth grade Algebra. And find out early if there are middle school classes that may be included on your high school transcript.

EXTRA CREDIT

Don't pass up the chance for extra credit. Many teachers offer extra credit early in the semester, before you know if you need it.

My youngest son had a chance to make an extra credit poster about a book he had read in his Advanced Placement Literature class. He already had a 98% in the class and was debating whether to make the poster. I reminded him that finals were still on the horizon and giving himself a bit more cushion could pay off if some unforeseen disaster happened to occur during finals week.

Ironically, he came down with the flu. Getting prepared for finals was a bit harder with the coughing, sneezing, wanting to stay in bed feeling. But with the extra credit and the hard work all semester, he did not have to stress about having less time and ability to prepare for finals.

Take advantage of the chance to give yourself a cushion by doing the extra credit when it comes around. You could be very glad you did as it may save your grade later on.

STUDY SESSIONS

Take advantage of study sessions. Many schools offer after school study sessions and often teachers will organize review sessions during the school year. These study sessions provide a great place to get more focused help and gain a greater understanding of which material the teacher considers most important. Make time to attend because a teacher directed study session will generally enable you to use your limited study time the most efficiently. Teachers create the class objectives and write the tests. When a teacher invites you to study with them, you can anticipate getting the most targeted and useful sort of help in understanding assignments and preparing for tests.

EYES ON THE PRIZE

Keep your eye on the prize. Remind yourself that your goal is to get into the college of your choice and to earn scholarships to pay for it. Find creative ways to keep your goal in mind at all times. Perhaps make a sign and put it on your bedroom door or bathroom mirror. What better way to keep your focus.

My goal is a 4.0 this semester!

AMAZING GRADES CHECKLIST

- [ ] Set a Goal

- [ ] Let your teachers know your goal

- [ ] Get a planner (and use it)

- [ ] Do the extra credit

- [ ] Attend study sessions offered by teachers

14 SCHOLARSHIP SUCCESS

CHAPTER 3

FOR FRESHMEN (AND 8TH GRADERS)

THE CLASSES

While every high school will offer different classes, you need to select the classes that match up with the requirements of the college you wish to attend. In addition, you will want to take classes that give you the best preparation for getting admitted and getting scholarships. Read on to find out what those classes are.

KNOW THE REQUIRED CLASSES

Many colleges publish a list of classes they expect you to have taken when you come out of high school. For example, according to the

University of California Admissions office, students applying for admission in 2015 must have these courses (or replacement test scores in some cases) to even be considered.[1]

- History/Social Science - 2 years
- College preparatory English - 4 years
- Mathematics - 3 years (4 recommended)
- Laboratory Science - 2 years (3 recommended) covering biology, chemistry & physics.
- Language other than English - 2 years (or equivalent)
- Visual & Performing arts - 1 year
- College Preparatory Elective - 1 year

Most universities will have a list very similar to this one. Take time to look up the high school class requirements for the colleges you want to attend. Knowing what is expected when you begin choosing classes as a high school freshman will help ensure that you

---

[1] University of California Berkeley. (2015) Retrieved from http://admission.universityofcalifornia.edu/freshman/requirements/index.html

don't accidentally take yourself out of the running for the school of your choice.

TAKE ADVANCED CLASSES

A 2011 study by the National Association of College Admissions Counseling (NACAC) asked 1263 colleges to indicate what they considered first in choosing to admit students.[2]

What do Colleges consider most Important?				
Factor's Importance	Very	Moderate	Limited	None
Grades in college prep courses	84.3%	11.9%	2.3%	1.5%
Strength of curriculum	67.7	20.4	5.8	6.2
Admission test (SAT/ACT)	59.2	29.6	6.9	4.2
Grades in all courses	51.9	39.2	6.9	1.9
SOURCE: NACAC ADMISSIONS TRENDS SURVEY 2011				

Does it surprise you that they're looking at your grades? And more importantly, they are looking at the grades you got in the classes

---

[2] National Association for College Admission Counseling. (2011) *Admission Trends Survey*.retrieved from http://www.nacacnet.org/studentinfo/articles/Pages/Factors-in-the-Admission-Decision.aspx

they list on their website as required for you to get admitted.

You may be wondering, "what does a college admissions adviser consider a college preparatory course?

The answer might be different for every school, but here are some clues. Many high schools offer advanced classes. Sometimes a school will label them "Honors" classes. Other schools call them "Advanced Placement (AP) courses" or "International Baccalaureate (IB) classes." When colleges say they place importance on the "strength of your curriculum" you can interpret that to mean they are checking to see if you took classes in some of these categories.

This spring, when you and your friends start to talk about which classes to take in the coming year, remember that if your school offers advanced classes, you will benefit from taking Honors, or Advanced Placement, or whatever your school is calling the college preparatory track.

The AP and IB programs requires students

to take a test at the end of the school year to demonstrate they have learned the material. Not only do colleges want to see these on your high school transcript, but they will often give you college credit for your work in your high school AP and IB classes.

The AP program also gives honors and awards to students who take multiple tests and achieve passing scores. If you are serious about excelling in your AP classes, you will improve your chances of getting into the

Criteria for Advanced Placement Awards

Award	Criteria
AP Scholar	3 or higher on 3 or more AP exams
AP Scholar with Honor	3.25 average score on all exams and 3 or higher on 5 or more
AP Scholar with Distinction	3.5 average score on all AP exams taken and 3 or higher on 5 or more
State AP Scholar	1 male and 1 female in each state with the highest average (above 3) on the greatest number of AP exams
National AP Scholar	4 or higher average on all AP exams taken and 4 or higher on at least eight or more of these exams.

PROFESSIONALS.COLLEGEBOARD.COM/K-12/AP-SCHOLAR

college of your choice and you will earn an award that can be listed in the "Honors, Awards & Achievements" section of your scholarship applications (see page 28).

In addition, because Advanced Placement (AP) or International Baccalaureate (IB) courses are measured by a standardized final test, they therefore provide admissions committees and scholarship committees an additional method to compare students from different schools. For this reason, some colleges give extra consideration during the admissions process to students taking these courses.

Getting an awesome GPA is essential, but not enough on it's own. A college admissions counselor wants to see that you did well in the list of classes they consider essential for college. And according to the 2011 NACAC study, they are looking to see if your great GPA is based primarily on college preparatory coursework (and NOT an overabundance of physical education courses or the infamous underwater basket weaving).

THE CLASSES   21

22   SCHOLARSHIP SUCCESS

CHAPTER 4

FOR FRESHMEN

THE LISTS

Every college application and scholarship application you encounter will ask you to list certain experiences you have had throughout your high school years.

VOLUNTEER COMMUNITY SERVICE
HONORS, AWARDS & ACHIEVEMENTS
LEADERSHIP EXPERIENCE
EXTRACURRICULAR ACTIVITIES & INTERESTS
WORK EXPERIENCE

Just imagine if you sit down to fill out the application for the school of your dreams and the only community service you can recall is the canned food drive you helped with two weeks ago. Of course you will be involved in many activities during your four years of high school. However, when you are trying to list your freshman activities during the last semester of your senior year, chances are you will forget something. And even if you remember EVERYTHING, you likely won't recall all the detail about the dates, times and places, which is often just what a scholarship application requires.

>Solution to your memory deficiency... Make a list (or several lists)...to keep track of all you do!

If you are good at keeping records online, your LISTS can be a file on your computer or on your phone. If you are the kind of person who likes to jot things down with paper and pencil, the list can be a piece of paper pinned to your bathroom mirror or the pages provided in the back of this little book. You will find space to make your lists, starting on page 86 of this book.

VOLUNTEER COMMUNITY SERVICE

Virtually every college application and

scholarship application you encounter will ask you to list your volunteer community service efforts. Quite possibly you're already keeping a list if your school also requires a certain number of community service hours.

You will have performed many hours of community service from the time you enter high school to the time you apply for college, but you won't remember when, or where, or what. So start a list today. If you're having a hard time finding opportunities to serve, look within the clubs, teams, and organizations to which you already belong.

Local organizations such as libraries, hospitals, homeless shelters and community parks often need volunteers as well. Some communities have websites

UNITEDWAY.ORG AND **JUSTSERVE.ORG** ARE TWO WEBSITES THAT ENABLE YOU TO SEARCH FOR COMMUNITY VOLUNTEER OPPORTUNITIES BY ZIP CODE.

THE LISTS   25

that list volunteer opportunities. In addition, some school classes and activities involve community service. Perhaps your school offers a tutoring class, or the opportunity to volunteer as a teacher's aid or the manager for a sports team. These activities provide service for others in your school community.

Write down every time you participate in community service. Make a note of where you serve, what date, and for how long. You also

> **Community Service**
>
> re-shelving books at the library, once a week June thru Aug. 2013 (about 35 hours) - Mrs. Mogen supervised
>
> Scouting for food drive - every November (about 12 hours) - Scoutmasters Romney and Slack in charge
>
> Helped with homeless meal under the bridge 4 Wednesdays in January 2014 - abt. 10 hours. Mom in charge.

might want to make a note of the adults who are there, just in case you need someone to verify your participation. If you want to flip to page 86 you can start your list right now.

Wherever you put your list, just be sure to write down every time you volunteer at the local library or hospital, clear trails at the park, entertain residents at a senior center, deliver food to the homeless, weed the community gardens, or help organize a church fund-raiser. The list will remind you that volunteer community service is essential for getting scholarships. If you hang your list where you see it all the time, you might find yourself motivated to do more community service.

Most applications want a list of community service activities starting from the time you begin high school, so be sure to get your list started at the end of eighth grade. Don't forget we've provided a place for you to start your list on page 86 of this book.

And while you are making lists, you will want

to keep track of a few other things almost every scholarship application will request. Read on to find out exactly what else scholarship applications want you to list.

HONORS, AWARDS & ACHIEVEMENTS

Scholarship committees like to hear about the great things that other organizations have discovered about you. When you get involved and give of your time to a club or community organization, often you are rewarded for your efforts. Awards and honors can come from many places: community involvement, school activities, science or math competitions, dance, music, drama, athletics, church involvement, community service clubs and more. Community service clubs such as Boy Scouts of America, Key club and Honor Society exist in almost every community.

Talk to your friends or neighbors. Find out if they know about a chapter for any of these organizations in your area. If you know of kids who are a few years older than you, talk to them about activities they have chosen which provide opportunities to earn recognition for your talents, abilities, and efforts. If necessary, search the Internet for ideas where you can get involved.

We all have certain activities we prefer over all others. Sometimes, you find a lot of your time gobbled up by just one or two things you love. Perhaps you love to spend all your time in dance class and dance related activities. However, being aware that your goal is to build a stellar scholarship resume can help motivate you to get involved in a wider range of activities.

Honor Received	Date	From?
A.P. Scholar with Distinction	Dec 2015	College Board A.P. Program
Eagle Scout	Jun 2014	Boy Scouts of America
Most Inspirational Runner	Sep 2015	School Cross Country Team

TRY NEW THINGS

If you expand your range of activities to include a wider variety, you will find other things you like and build yourself a better scholarship resume in the process.

My three sons love to Pole Vault. They spend a lot of time vaulting or training to vault. And yet, when it comes to listing your achievements on a scholarship application, pole vault may not give you a very long list.

ASK YOUR TEACHERS

Amidst their love of vaulting, my children diversified. In many cases, the opportunities came to them through school teachers. My oldest son built and raced a CO_2 car during his early years of high school. Receiving recognition for the design and speed of the car became something he could list on his applications. My youngest son received a Washington State award for a science project that was part of his required freshman science class. His teacher helped the project team to learn where they could submit their work. When he began his scholarship applications, he was grateful to have kept the details of that award in a place where he could use the information.

SEARCH THE INTERNET

With the increased support by businesses for the STEM (Science, Technology, Engineering, Math) related disciplines, you can always find a place to be involved, and to receive recognition. A little bit of digging will turn up competitions in your area, writing contests you can enter online, and much more. Ask your teachers or browse the Internet for opportunities to receive recognition for the work you're already doing in science, math, writing or other classes.

Expand your involvement to activities outside of school as well. All my kids participated in church youth groups and my sons in the Boy Scouts of America. In addition to being able to list church and scouting awards, they also found many community service and leadership opportunities to include.

Being involved, and keeping track of those times when you are recognized for your contribution will significantly increase your ability to present a very powerful scholarship application when the time comes. If you want to keep track of your honors, awards and achievements in this little book, you will find a place to do that on page 87.

LEADERSHIP EXPERIENCE

Leadership can be defined as the act of guiding or directing a group, exerting social influence to bring out the best in others, and motivating others to the highest levels of performance. Maybe your school is small and getting involved is easy. Maybe your school has more than 2000 people and getting elected to any student body office is nearly impossible.

I remember running for class president in high school, and losing. But I still found plenty to list on my scholarship applications under the category of leadership.

> YOU DON'T HAVE TO BE ELECTED TO BE A LEADER!

Being elected by your classmates or receiving a leadership title is not the only way to gain leadership experience during your school years. You can find many different opportunities to get leadership experience and you will be glad when you do. Almost all school clubs select individuals to fill leadership roles. School clubs such as Future Business Leaders

Position Held & Resonsibilities	Organization	Date
Vice President	Honor Society	2014-2015
Team Captain	Cross Country Team	2014-2015
Troop Photographer	Troop 408, Boy Scouts	Jan - Dec 2013

of America (FBLA) offer leadership training and provide great leadership experiences. Some schools have a leadership class and anyone can sign up.

Outside of school, many organizations provide chances to lead. Churches, youth groups, scout troops and service clubs give young people a chance to be leaders.

If you have a job, look carefully at your work activities to identify the times when you are filling a leadership role in your work. Perhaps even talk with your supervisor. Let him or her know your goal, and ask about leadership opportunities that could be made available to you.

Being aware that leadership is an important part of earning scholarships will help you be on the look-out for opportunities, and make you more likely to recognize them when they come along. On page 88 in the back of this book you can record your leadership experiences as they happen.

ACTIVITIES & INTERESTS

Think ahead about how you expect to spend

your time in your four years of high school. If your list would only include one flavor of activities, you might want to work at diversifying.

Professionals such as coaches, marching band instructors, and drama teachers generally feel very passionate about their particular discipline. It is not uncommon for a student to feel a strong influence pulling them to spend all their time in one particular type of activity. Knowing the value of getting involved in a variety of activities will help you avoid the shock and despair that can come when you sit down to a scholarship application and discover, too late, that you really don't have much variety in your list.

Activity	Organization	Date
Varsity Basketball	Riverside High School	2012-2015
Summer Basketball Camp	Washington State Univ.	2013-2014
Hoopfest Basketball Tourney	City of Spokane	2012-2014

Juggling school work with all the other things that will fill your list can be a challenge, but choose wisely a set of activities that will help you become a well-rounded person, and you will have no problem creating a strong list of extracurricular activities for your applications. Start that list today, in the space provided for you on page 89 in this book.

WORK EXPERIENCE

Even though getting into college is your main job right now, a scholarship application with a blank "Work Experience" section probably will not float to the top of the pile. Some students find they want or need to work during the school year. Others find they can work during the summer. Whenever you work, keep track of what you have done.

Nature of Work	Employer	Hours	Dates
landscaping	Riverside School District	250 hrs	June thru Aug 2015
soccer referee	Sunnyvale Soccer club	110 hrs	Aug 2103 - May 2014

Make a list that includes your employer, the type of work you did, the date or date range in which you performed the work, and about how many hours you worked in each place of employment.

And remember there are activities that can count as work, even if you did not receive payment for the effort. When we have a major work project at home, such as clearing debris from the creek, or building a bridge, or putting in a sprinkler system, we may or may not pay our kids when they help. But either way, those hours can be listed as work experience.

If you turn to the table entitled "WORK EXPERIENCE" on page 90 you can jot down any work experience you have already had.

It takes a bit of self discipline to keep track of community service, extracurricular activities and work experience through your four years of high school. You have to make time to write down these experiences, along with the leadership, honors, and awards along the way.

JUST DO IT! I guarantee you will be so

happy that you took the time. At one point in my youngest son's senior year he had ten scholarship applications in various stages of completion. Of the ten applications, all of them asked him to list information in at least three of these list categories and some in all five areas. These lists will allow you to speed through this part of any application, making it possible to complete many more applications in the time you have available.

ONE MORE LIST - STEM ACTIVITIES

If you love building things, taking things apart, or discovering how things work, you may be headed for an education in science, technology, engineering or mathematics (STEM).

If there is even a remote possibility that you will plan to study in a field related to these education categories, then be sure to search for scholarships designed to support STEM education. And be sure to keep a list of your science related activities.

Over the past couple decades, a growing concern has evolved that the United States is not educating enough college graduates in careers related to science, technology, engineering and math. To address this concern, the federal government has allotted significant financial resources to the National Science Foundation, the Department of Education and the Department of Health and Human Services.

As an example, in 2011 the National Science Foundation received $6.913 billion dollars in appropriations from the US Congress to promote STEM education. This number represents a $1.543 billion increase since 2003.[1]

In turn, these federal agencies find ways to encourage corporations, local government agencies, schools and non-profit organizations to promote STEM education. In the case of the National Science Foundation, their federal funding is given as grants to organizations who can demonstrate their efforts to support STEM education. In many cases this grant money is used to fund scholarships.

---

[1] Gonzalez, Heather B., "An Analysis of STEM Education Funding at NSF: Trends and Policy Discussion." Congressional Research Service R42470, 12 Dec. 2012. Web. 17 Feb. 2015

In order to be prepared to show your interest and involvement in STEM related learning activities, you will want to add one more list to your list of lists. Keep track of every time you build a model rocket or a potato launcher. Look for chances to get involved in STEM related competitions. Many schools have science fairs on a local level, but there are also national events to be found with a bit of searching.

My youngest son participated in a competition sponsored by the United States Army Educational Outreach Program. He and his classmates made a water wheel designed to generate electricity. They were recognized as "state champions" for their work.

He also designed and built a pole vault training apparatus at his high school. These science related activities have given him some great line items to

THE LISTS   41

include in his list of STEM activities.

Write down any competitions, workshops or classes you attend (Science Olympiad, Math is Cool, Science related Merit Badge clinics, H_2O Car Racing, etc.) If you help design or build a structure for a service project, write it down. If you help with home repairs that involve electrical or the use of math and design skills, this type of activity could be included. You can start your STEM Related Activities list on page 91.

Your list of STEM activities will come in handy when you begin filling out scholarship applications for those considering an education in fields related to science and technology.

Whether your interests lie in science, languages, music, politics or any other area of study, you will need your lists to successfully complete the scholarship applications to help pay for your studies. Be diligent in writing down these experiences and it will pay off in a big way. And remember we've provided space for you to begin building all your lists today. See page 86 in this book to get started.

LIST CHECKLIST

Start your lists when you start high school.

- [ ] Volunteer Community Service
- [ ] Honors, Awards & Achievements
- [ ] Leadership Experience
- [ ] Activities & Interests
- [ ] Work Experience
- [ ] STEM Related Activities

SCHOLARSHIP SUCCESS

CHAPTER 5

FOR SOPHOMORES

THE TESTS

Only one piece of data allows college admissions officers and scholarship committees to compare you to all the other applications in the pile. That piece of information is your standardized test score.

> A REALLY GOOD TEST SCORE CAN OPEN THE DOOR TO ACCEPTANCE, TUITION ASSISTANCE AND SCHOLARSHIPS.

The SAT and the ACT are the two standardized test scores requested by most universities.

Scholarship committees and college admissions departments take into account standardized tests as a way of comparing student applicants from schools and education systems all over the world.[1]

	ACT	SAT
Stanford	30-36 range for top 88% admitted.	700-800 range (per category) for top 70% admitted
U of Michigan	30-33 range for those admitted.	650-770 range (per category) for those admitted
Brigham Young University	28.3 - average score of those admitted.	640-655 average range (per category) for those admitted
U of North Carolina	28-33 range for those admitted.	600-700 average range (per category) for those admitted
Princeton	31-35 range of middle 50% admitted	690-800 range (per category) for middle 50% admitted
U of California Berkeley	32 - average score of those admitted	708 average score (per category) for students admitted
2014 Freshman Profile Test Score Averages		

---

1 http://admission.stanford.edu/basics/selection/profile.html
http://admissions.umich.edu/apply/freshmen-applicants/admitted-student-profile
http://yfacts.byu.edu/Article?id=143
http://admissions.unc.edu/apply/class-profile/
http://www.princeton.edu/pub/profile/admission/undergraduate/
http://admissions.berkeley.edu/studentprofile

With a quick online search, including keywords such as "freshman profile" you can discover the test scores for students who got accepted to the schools you are considering.

For example, to see test score data for the class of 2014 from Princeton, just type this string into your search engine:

Princeton Freshman Profile 2014

Not only do the schools publish test scores, but some post information telling applicants what scholarship they will receive if their test scores are in a certain range. Brigham Young University is one example. A scholarship matrix posted on their website indicates students applying for the 2015 school year can receive a scholarship to cover part or all of their tuition if they meet a certain GPA standard and if they score 31 or above on the ACT.[2] Another example can be found on the website for the University of Nevada, Reno (UNR). UNR awards $5,000 per year —for

---

2 https://financialaid.byu.edu/sites/financialaid.byu.edu/files/files/New%20Freshman%20Scholarship%20Matrix%202015-16.pdf

four years total— in tuition scholarships to anyone with a 3.50 GPA (or higher) and at least 31 on the ACT.[3] From these examples, you can see the value of a strong test score.

Some sources may lead you to believe that a good test score requires exorbitant amounts of time and money spent on tutoring, but don't buy it! The resources to help you prepare for and perform well are mostly free and at your fingertips if you are willing to make the effort. As you read through his chapter, you will learn about these free resources and discover how you can take advantage of them.

So what can you do to get the test score that will open these doors to acceptance and scholarship opportunities for you? I recommend three basic steps.

>   TAKE THE TEST EARLY

>   TAKE THE TEST TWICE

>   KNOW THE TEST

These three actions may sound simple, and

---

3 http://www.unr.edu/financial-aid/understanding-financial-aid/scholarships/university-scholarships

they are. But these actions are also key to a great test score. If you get started early and follow the recommendations in this chapter, you can accomplish all of these steps with very little trouble.

TAKE THE TEST EARLY

My oldest children are twins, a boy and a girl. And while they exhibited signs of intelligence from a young age, you can tell from this photo that early on in life academics were not a high priority.

THE TESTS 49

However, as they entered middle school, we talked about the importance of good grades and good preparation for testing.

At the local middle school one of the teachers helped coordinate the Johns Hopkins Talent Search which encouraged taking the SAT test before high school. There are a variety of programs that encourage students to take these tests early which is a good thing.

However, some lead you to believe you must pay their fee (in addition to the test registration fee), but don't be fooled. If you are offered the chance to participate in a program that encourages you to take the ACT or SAT early, find out enough about it to know if the benefits being offered have value to you, and are worth the price being asked. Those programs that require additional fees over and above the cost of the test registration will sometimes provide the opportunity to be associated with a specific organization or group, but also generally result in direct mail or email offers to spend money on resources that can often be accessed for free.

We learned by our fourth child, that anyone can sign up to take these tests without paying an extra fee. To register for the test, simply visit the official website and select the test date that works for you.

HTTP://SAT.COLLEGEBOARD.ORG/

HTTP://WWW.ACTSTUDENT.ORG

In our family, four of the kids took the SAT as seventh graders just to get a sense of what standardized testing is all about. And all of our kids have taken the ACT as sophomores.

Taking the test in the early years of high school has several advantages. First, you get familiar with the test. This familiarity will make it easier for you to relax if you return to take it a second time. Second, you get a benchmark score, and an idea of what you need to do to achieve the score you're aiming to earn. Third, you encounter subject matter that you've recently learned.

The SAT and ACT tests include subject matter that is learned in the first couple years of high school. For example, the math portion will cover concepts such as fractions, decimals, ratios, averages, and order of operations. Consequently, taking the test as a sophomore can be a benefit. You will study these concepts in eighth, ninth, and tenth grade so why wait until your senior year to show what you know on the standardized test?

TAKE THE TEST TWICE

Some students find once is enough for the ACT or SAT. Most however, will take the test more than once. Statistics indicate that the chances of improving your score are very good. Both the ACT and SAT organizations publish information to illustrate what percentage of students improve their test score the second time around.[4]

ACT	SAT
57% of 2013 graduating class increased their composite score on a retest.	55% of seniors in 2014 increased their score from the test taken their junior year.

4 http://professionals.collegeboard.com/testing/sat-reasoning/scores/retake
http://www.actstudent.org/faq/more.html

In high school, the twins took Geometry as freshmen. Being aware that the math portion of the ACT test covers concepts taught in Algebra and Geometry, we encouraged them to take the ACT as sophomores. With scores of 30 and 33 respectively, they were thrilled. And yet when we pulled out the scholarship matrix for the school they hoped to attend, we found that 30 was not quite high enough to get a full tuition scholarship.

My husband, seeing the dollar value of a

review + retest + $500 ≥ 33

33 on ACT = full tuition scholarship

Net gain = FULL TUITION

SOLID INVESTMENT

higher test score, offered our daughter $500 if she would retake the test and get a 33. Her twin brother, ever the entrepreneur, asked, "What will I get if I retake the test and get a 36?" Thinking this was near to impossible (because 36 is the highest score possible) my husband agreed to pay him as well.

By this time, our kids were seniors. They hadn't been in Algebra or Geometry for a couple years. However, they both had seen two more years of English and in our son's case, a lot more science. They both registered for a second try at the ACT early in their senior year.

> So, you're wondering - Does she get the $500?
>
> Does he get the perfect score?

If you plan to take the SAT or ACT in your senior year, one thing to remember is the deadline established by the school you plan to attend. Some schools will not consider scores for tests taken after December when they evaluate your application for admission and for scholarships. Another important consideration is to take the test early enough in your senior year that you get your score back in time to put it on your scholarship applications. My youngest son found he had already filled out two scholarship applications before he received his second set of test scores. Because his score had gone from a 34 to a 35 he wished he had been able to include it.

KNOW THE TEST

What do you need to know about the test to be successful? First, you need to know which test and what parts of the test are required by the schools where you will apply. Second, and most importantly, knowing the content, format, structure and scoring methodology is key to being efficient during a timed standardized test.

KNOW WHAT PARTS ARE REQUIRED

While many schools will accept scores from either the ACT or the SAT, some require one or the other. In addition, the ACT has an optional writing section that is required by some schools. And the SAT offers optional "subject tests" that are required by many universities. For example, Northwestern

University in Illinois requires the ACT writing section. And for students who have been home-schooled they also require an SAT subject test in Math and 2 other subjects.

When you register for the test, make sure you know what is required at the schools you may attend. If several subject tests are required you may want to spread out the testing dates to give yourself the best chance of doing well on each.

KNOW THE CONTENT

Test content preparation can be as simple as doing your homework and paying attention in class. There are many online resources for sample test problems to help you review material that is likely to appear on the test.

The official web site for each test can be a FANTASTIC FREE resource.

HTTP://SAT.COLLEGEBOARD.ORG/

HTTP://WWW.ACTSTUDENT.ORG

You'll find free sample questions, updates on

what has changed in the test, and many other tools to help you get familiar with the type of test questions you can expect to encounter.

Many organizations offer study guides and online tools for sale, but before you purchase anything, check out what you can find for free.

Our daughter spent several hours in the weeks leading up to the test reviewing and practicing math problems. Doing practice problems can benefit a student in multiple ways. First, you see some of the test content presented in the way it will appear on the test. Second, you encounter the type of problems you can expect to see on the test. As you practice more and more, the different question styles become familiar, and your ability to move quickly through the test increases.

Unlike his twin sister, our son did not begin his review until the night before the test. We had purchased a review book as a Christmas gift for his sister, and he looked at review problems the night before the exam. However, with the academic effort both twins had made in their school courses, they felt prepared. Both kids also felt confident and comfortable about the test because they had taken it before. The structure and format were familiar.

KNOW THE STRUCTURE AND FORMAT

We all know people who seem to be natural born test takers, but most of us are not. If you feel your test taking abilities are not extremely strong, then it is crucial for you to get familiar with the test format so you can avoid running out of time. Being familiar with the format and structure will allow you to relax and work more efficiently during the allotted time.

The test is divided into sections. The test is timed. Visit the official websites for the ACT and SAT tests (page 57) to find additional detail about what each section contains and how many minutes are allotted per section.

Standardized test designers are very good at making multiple choice answers seem like they could be right. Spending time with

SAT TEST STRUCTURE

Section	Time	Questions
Reading	70 minutes	48 passage based
		19 sentence completion
Math	70 minutes	44 multiple choice
		10 solve for answer
Writing	60 minutes	25 improving sentences
		18 identifying errors
		6 improving paragraphs
		1 Essay
+ 20 different optional subject tests		

HTTP://SAT.COLLEGEBOARD.ORG/

sample problems will help you become familiar with the way questions and answers are structured and worded. You will develop the ability to more quickly understand what is being asked.

Taking time to discover strategies that will help you successfully navigate the various

ACT TEST STRUCTURE

Section	Time	Questions
English	45 minutes	75 questions
Math	60 minutes	60 questions
Reading	35 minutes	40 questions
Science	35 minutes	40 questions
Optional Writing	1 prompt	30 minutes

HTTP://WWW.ACTSTUDENT.ORG

sections can pay off as well. Many excellent review resources are offered for free through websites and mobile apps. One such resource is an app on your phone, designed to give you daily opportunities to review. To find a wealth of free review resources, try out these suggestions for some possible Internet searches:

SAMPLE SAT QUESTIONS

GUESSING STRATEGIES ON THE ACT

TIPS FOR TAKING THE ACT

FREE SAT PRACTICE TEST

HOW TO PREPARE FOR THE ACT MATH

SAT QUESTION OF THE DAY

MOBILE APPS FOR ACT REVIEW

Case in point, when my youngest son returned from taking the ACT a second time, I asked if his review efforts had been helpful. "YES!" was the answer. In his review, he came across a recommendation to scan for key words in the Reading Comprehension section. This strategy enabled him to maximize his efficiency and get through all the questions without running out of time.

TO GUESS OR NOT?

Of course you hope to be so prepared that

finishing each section in the allotted time will not be a problem for you. However, even the best test takers encounter situations where they just run out of time. If you know the scoring methodology for the test you are taking, you will be better prepared to respond when time gets short.

GUESSING ON THE SAT

On the SAT guessing wrong has been penalized for years in some sections. If you take the test before the spring of 2016, a wrong answer results in the subtraction of 1/4 point. For this reason, guessing can be more harmful than leaving a question blank.

> STARTING IN THE SPRING OF 2016, THERE WILL NO LONGER BE A PENALTY FOR GUESSING ON THE SAT.

However, there still may be value in guessing. Strategies exist that are likely to yield a net positive result if you guess on a batch of SAT questions.

Suppose you have twelve SAT questions in a single section for which you simply do not know answer. If you can eliminate one or two of the choices for each question, the statistical odds of getting a correct answer jump up. And now, guessing randomly, you've increased your chances of getting a few points to counter the potential for losing ¼ point on those that are wrong. It only takes three correct answers out of twelve to end up with a net positive ¾ point.

GUESSING ON THE ACT

For the ACT test, when in doubt, guessing is wise. Wrong answers do not have a scoring penalty on the ACT. If there are questions you cannot figure out, your best strategy for the ACT is to make a guess.

THE GOOD GUESS

If you have to GUESS, make it GOOD. Take a few seconds and attempt to eliminate one or more of the choices, thus increasing your chance of guessing correctly. If you run out of time to attempt elimination consider filling in the same letter for all remaining problems. In any multiple choice test, the answer is not going to always be A. It is more likely to be a random distribution of all the choices. For this reason, some experts recommend that if you guess by choosing the same letter for ten problems, you have a better chance of getting a few right than if you randomly select letters at the risk getting them ALL wrong.

And while you can do your research on the best way to guess, I recommend that your time will be better spent preparing to cruise through the test questions efficiently so guessing doesn't even become an issue.

Back to the story – Does Dad pay one twin? or two?

So the twins took the test for the second time. Both returned from the morning feeling confident they'd done well and anxious for the day when the test scores would be released. A few weeks later, about 5:30 in the morning, my husband and I were jolted from sleep by an ear piercing shriek. Leaping out of bed and rushing up the stairs I found my oldest son staring at a perfect score of 36 on the ACT. His work paid off in scholarships that would cover all his tuition and expenses for four years.

My daughter also improved her score enough to get a full tuition scholarship. The money my husband paid to each of the twins for their efforts in getting great test scores was

$750 FROM DAD + SCHOLARSHIPS TO COVER ALL TUITION & EXPENSES FOR 4 YEARS!

$500 FROM DAD + FULL TUITION FROM THE UNIVERSITY!

HAPPY PARENTS!

one of the best investments we ever made. A great test score is worth the work.

In summary, the time you put in before taking the test will greatly impact your score. Even if your Dad doesn't offer you money, just follow the steps outlined in this chapter and get the score you need to help you with your college admissions and scholarship success. You'll be glad you did!

STANDARDIZED TEST PREP CHECKLIST

☐ Get started early.

☐ Plan to take the test twice

☐ Check the test & deadline required by schools

☐ Review the format, content and structure

☐ Do LOTS of practice problems

68 SCHOLARSHIP SUCCESS

CHAPTER 6

FOR JUNIORS & SENIORS

THE SCHOLARSHIPS

You are ready. You have your great test score, your awesome GPA, and your lists, reminding you of all the fantastic activities you've been involved in during your high school years.

Now is the time to find those applications, fill them out, and send them in.

While many scholarship applications have a deadline in the spring of your senior year, don't wait until then to

> **DON'T WAIT** UNTIL YOU ARE A SENIOR TO START LOOKING. SOME SCHOLARSHIP APPLICATIONS MUST BE COMPLETED IN THE JUNIOR YEAR.

start looking. My kids have found a few that come due in December, or even in the Junior year. If you start your search early you won't miss out.

FINDING SCHOLARSHIPS

Now where are the scholarship applications? Some are easy to find, and some are more elusive. I recall sitting at the state championship basketball game when my middle son was a senior. I looked across the court and saw a huge banner, announcing a scholarship available to juniors. Too late, I thought, for him and most of the kids out on the court. But not too late for my junior and freshman. I quickly jotted down the website. Not all scholarships will show up in front of your face on a ten foot banner. You will have to do some looking, but here are the best places to start.

YOUR SCHOOL COUNSELOR

The counselor's office at your school will be receiving scholarship notifications regularly throughout the school year. Check in with your counselor as early as fall of your junior year, so you don't miss out on anything. There are a few applications that come due before your senior year even starts. But most will be available in the last 6 months of your senior year. And most will be due between December and March.

COMMUNITY RESOURCES

Every community is different, but you'll find that many organizations in your home town want to help and support young people in getting an education.

Public libraries often post scholarship opportunities. I recently walked into the library and saw a poster advertising a great scholarship offered by the John F. Kennedy Library Foundation. Applicants were asked to write an essay about an elected official who had the courage to stand for his or beliefs. Awards ranged from $500 to $5000. Make time to drop in occasionally and check the library bulletin board. You will be amazed by how many organizations want to help pay for your college education.

Nonprofit organizations associated with large corporations often have scholarship programs, especially technology companies seeking to encourage the study of science,

THE SCHOLARSHIPS   71

technology, engineering and math (STEM). Sometimes the programs are specific to employees but often they are open to everyone.

Employers frequently have scholarship programs available to the children of their employees. Check with your parents. Do they work for a company that offers scholarships? These are often a great return on the time investment required to complete the application. My children received scholarships each from their dad's employer, and the application was relatively quick compared to many others.

Service Clubs such as Kiwanis, Elks, Lions or Rotary often have scholarship programs within each local chapter, as well as some national programs. My youngest son completed a single application to the local Elks Lodge and received three scholarships — a local, state, and national scholarship from this generous service club.

These organizations generally want you to write essays, and the essays can be time consuming. But don't get discouraged because the time investment will pay off.

Even if the application takes a good deal of time, think of it this way. If you spend 4 hours writing an essay for an application that results in a $1000 scholarship, you are working at a pretty good hourly rate.

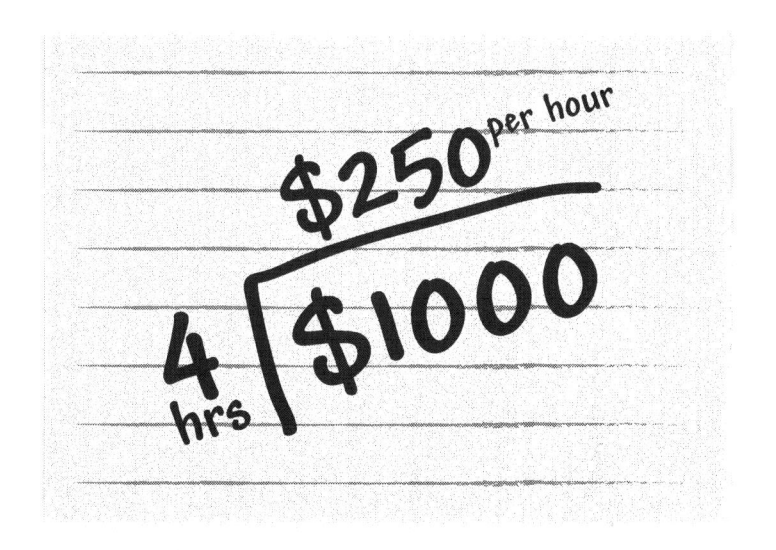

$$4_{hrs} \overline{)\$1000} = \$250 \text{ per hour}$$

The alternative could be getting a job on campus, at $10 per hour, to help pay for your education. I'd say writing the essay is worth the time. And if you save every essay, you may find the chance to use it again on another scholarship application.

Athletic and recreational associations often have scholarship programs. Consider groups such as bowling clubs, snowmobiling associations and especially state athletics associations. Within your own school, you may find that the Booster Club or individual teams have scholarships. Ask your coaches and the athletic director what they might know about scholarship opportunities.

UPPER CLASS-MEN

The printed graduation program is a great place to find ideas. Many schools make a list of all the scholarships the graduating seniors

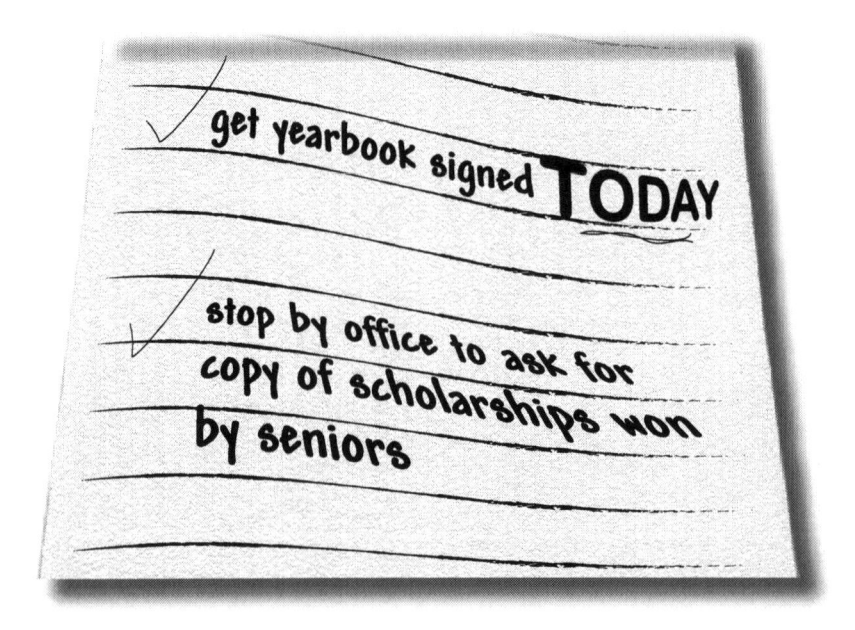

> ✓ get yearbook signed TODAY
>
> ✓ stop by office to ask for copy of scholarships won by seniors

have received. Getting a copy of that list gives you a great way to identify scholarships that might not be advertised online. In addition, the list contains scholarships proven to be winnable by someone from your school. If you aren't able to get a copy of the graduation program, stop by the office of your school before summer starts and ask for the list.

In addition you can contact other high schools in your area, or search their websites for a similar list.

ONLINE SEARCHES

Searching online will quickly help you discover some of what is out there. Scholarships come in all shapes and sizes. Some are for individuals pursuing a specific course of study, or who have a certain nationality or ethnic background. Others are for

> **VISIT ITUNES TO FIND MOBILE APP "SCHOLLY"** —A TOOL TO HELP LOCATE POTENTIAL SCHOLARSHIP OPPORTUNITIES.

individuals who have work experience in a certain area. For example, a scholarship exists for those students who have been golf caddies. Some are specific to a narrow geographic area. For instance, a scholarship exists in our region that requires the applicant to live within the boundaries of a certain Catholic parish. Other scholarships are open to individuals across the nation. The list goes on and on.

Don't get discouraged if you don't match the criteria for some scholarships. Keep searching until you identify those that match your qualifications. Here are some suggested search topics you can use on the internet to discover scholarships that are a good fit for you:

>   SCHOLARSHIPS FOR JUNIORS
>
>   STEM SCHOLARSHIPS AND CONTESTS
>
>   KIWANIS SCHOLARSHIPS (OR ELKS, ROTARY, ETC.)
>
>   NONPROFIT SCHOLARSHIP FOUNDATIONS
>
>   EWI (EXECUTIVE WOMEN INTERNATIONAL) - FOR THE GIRLS
>
>   SCHOLARSHIPS IN the name of your town or county

THE APPLICATIONS

You will likely plan to complete a lot of applications. At first it can seem overwhelming, but these strategies and steps will get you through a lot of applications in a rather efficient manner. As you search for scholarships, keep a list of those you find. Create a ranking system to identify the ones that you are the most excited about. By doing this, you will be sure to put your time toward the best possibilities first.

Elks ✶ *Top priority - due first - chance for local, state, and national*

Kootenai Electric *ALL about science - good shot. only one essay*

Kiwanis *lots of students from my school have gotten this one before!*

Kennedy Library Foundation *hard essay, national only, maybe won't do?*

Friends Of Pavillion Park *don't quite meet all the criteria - maybe or not?*

THE SCHOLARSHIPS

DEADLINES

Once you identify the applications you plan to complete, mark the deadlines on your calendar. This will help you plan ahead. You will be able to make sure you have enough time to get all the necessary pieces (transcripts, letters of recommendation, essays, and such) gathered and ready to go.

MARCH

2	3	4 engineering scholarship application due	5
9	10 Kootenai Electric App due	11	12
16	17	18 Kiwanis App Due	19

Keep your calendar in a spot where you take a glance at it often. This will help you prevent the accident of missing a deadline for those scholarships you hope to earn.

TRANSCRIPTS

Check which applications need transcripts and get them all ordered from your school early in the year. Order a few extra. Some organizations will want the transcript sealed, and others will not. Order them all sealed, because you can always open a transcript, but you can't seal it back up.

Schools can print your standardized test scores as part of your transcript, or on the back. You may have to ask them to do this. If you have plans to take the test during your senior year, do it early so you can get your test score to go with the sealed transcript you'll be submitting for scholarships.

CLASS RANK

While you're ordering your transcript, ask your school to tell you your class rank. Many scholarship applications require this information. Often class rank is included on the transcript, but if not you can ask your school to print the rank on the back of the transcript or on a separate paper included in the sealed document.

LETTERS OF RECOMMENDATION

Many applications will request letters of recommendation. When you ask a teacher or employer to write you a letter of recommendation, ask for a few extra signed copies. This enables you to have several on hand as you come upon additional applications.

SAVE, SAVE, SAVE AND REUSE!

Remember those lists you made. Every scholarship application will likely ask for that information in one form or another. Most applications will also require an essay of some sort. Your applications will most commonly be in a fillable PDF form. When you start on the application, **SAVE, SAVE, SAVE!**

And when you finish, if you copy the essays from your first applications and save them in a word document, you will very likely find you can modify and re-use the work in a later application. In addition, the lists you make of community service, work experience, and such can be re-used from one application to the next. If you copy and save the contents of each application you will find you get faster and faster at completing the next one.

And of course, the more scholarship applications you complete, the more scholarships you have a chance to win.

SCHOLARSHIP APPLICATION CHECKLIST

- [ ] Rank your applications in order of priority

- [ ] Mark your deadlines on the calendar

- [ ] Order transcripts (sealed) from your school

- [ ] Request letters of recommendation

- [ ] Save application contents for future re-use

82 SCHOLARSHIP SUCCESS

CHAPTER 7

FOR SENIORS

THE PAYOFF

It's time to celebrate.

You've earned the grades, you've achieved great test scores, you've filled out the applications with ease (because you kept such great lists all through high school).

Congratulations! Enjoy the thrill of getting that acceptance letter from the school of your choice. Have fun celebrating as those scholarship awards show up in the mailbox. Be grateful that your college experience will not require you to take on substantial debt.

BE GRATEFUL

And don't forget to send notes of appreciation to those organizations who have donated to support your education. Often scholarship committees are comprised of people you may know or have met in your community. Take time to express your gratitude for the work they do to make scholarships possible. Your sincere thank you note will brighten their day and encourage them to continue providing this service for many young people in years to come.

In addition, many service clubs don't stop at one scholarship. If you do your part, they may renew your scholarship every year that you are in college.

You should also be aware there are scholarships you can apply for during your college experience, some from the same organizations mentioned in this guide. But that is a discussion for another day. For now, enjoy your payoff!

COMMUNITY SERVICE

Nature of Service	Supervised by?	Total Hours	Dates

HONORS, AWARDS & ACHIEVEMENTS

Recognition Received	Received from?	Date

LEADERSHIP

Position Held & Responsibilities	Organization	Dates

EXTRACURRICULAR ACTIVITIES

Activity	Organization	Dates

MAKE YOUR LIST

WORK EXPERIENCE

Nature of Work	Employer	Total Hours	Dates
_____	_____	_____	_____
_____	_____	_____	_____
_____	_____	_____	_____
_____	_____	_____	_____
_____	_____	_____	_____
_____	_____	_____	_____
_____	_____	_____	_____
_____	_____	_____	_____
_____	_____	_____	_____
_____	_____	_____	_____

STEM RELATED ACTIVITIES

Activity	Dates

MAKE YOUR LIST

APPENDIX
FOR PARENTS

CLEAR THE PATH

While your students head down the path to success in college acceptance and scholarships, you will be busy keeping the path free of broken glass and prickly thorns. There are obstacles that can threaten to derail even the most committed, motivated student so here are some warnings.

KEEP AN EYE ON THE CURRICULUM

Federal and state policy makers like to legislate curriculum. Local school boards also seem to take an interest in shaking up the curriculum from time to time. On page 15 you will find a sample list of classes that every college applicant is required to take. Keep an eye on your school district to make sure they don't do something crazy, like taking Algebra out of the line-up, or replacing it with something they will call Algebra. You may have to attend school board meetings, form parent committees, and write letters to the editor, but do it for your kids.

DON'T LET THE KIDS GET OVERBOOKED

As the high school years begin, the opportunities to be involved expand exponentially. While there are scores of valuable, education enriching activities tempting the kids to get involved, you will want to help them keep their priorities in order. Grades should always be the top priority. Of over 1200 colleges surveyed, 84.3% said they look at grades before anything else. See page 17 for details on the study regarding this statistic. Help your student remember to make sure quality time goes to keeping up the grades as they head down the path of Key Club, Green Club, Chess Club, Robotics Club, and more.

STUDY THE SCHOOL OPTIONS

Your student will thank you for helping them avoid excessive college expenses by directing them in their choice of a fantastic AND affordable College or University.

We are blessed to live in a time when outstanding educational institutions exist in every corner of the country. Some have been here a lot longer than others, and many will argue the immense value of attending a long established institution; greater earning capability, more companies coming to recruit, better professors, and such. My husband attended three universities, including Stanford. While we are grateful for his degree from Stanford, he has often remarked that the academic rigor at Brigham Young University and San Jose State equaled (and in some cases surpassed) the classroom experience at Stanford University.

The bottom line is that your student can get a fantastic education and have great opportunities for employment at many schools which have reasonable tuition expenses.

There exists some unseen force in our society that will lead you to believe expensive trips to dozens of campuses around the country will be necessary in order to evaluate and select a school. Most colleges do have excellent and informative free tours for prospective students, and once you've narrowed your choice, taking a visit can be a good idea.

However, most of the information you need to gather can be found online. Here are some questions to start with in evaluating the education and future employment and earning opportunities associated with any school:

- Which schools offer the degree or degrees your student wants to pursue & the disciplines that will help them land a job?

- Have the various disciplines (accounting, engineering, business, etc.) been ranked by US News & World Report? You can go online to http://colleges.usnews.rankingsandreviews.com/best-colleges and type in the name of the college you're considering to see how it stacks up.

- What companies recruit at the university? A search under "Career Services" or "Jobs and Careers" for the schools of your choice will lead you to information about the companies that recruit at any given institution.

- Are graduates from this school getting jobs? And what is the placement percentage for graduates? Enter "Job Placement Statistics" and the school of your choice to find this information. In addition to the Universities themselves, there are a few websites that compile this sort of data.

- What is the twenty year "return on investment (ROI)" for the schools your student is considering. Annually published College ROI reports take into account the total cost of going to school, the salary progression over the twenty years after you graduate, and the total you get to keep after attacking student loans. This information can help a student see how the college of their choice may or may not put them in the best earning position in the long run.

Online you will find a wealth of data to help evaluate the various institutions of higher education. For example, a study conducted by Careerbuilder.com provides information regarding those degrees that were most sought after by employers in 2014.[1]

MOST SOUGHT AFTER GRADUATES

Business	39%
Computer & Information Sciences	28%
Engineering	18%
Math & Statistics	14%
Health Professions & Related Clinical Sciences	14%
Communications Technologies	12%
Engineering Technologies	11%
Education	7%
Liberal Arts & Sciences, General Studies, Humanities	10%
Science Technologies	7%
Communications & Journalism	7%
WWW.CAREERBUILDER.COM	

If you take the time to discover and discuss with your student the benefits and disadvantages of different schools, your student will have a great advantage. The selection of a college or university will be based on information rather than glossy promotional

---

[1] Grasz, Jennifer, "Most In-Demand Majors" CareerBuilder.com. Web. 20 Feb. 2015. http://www.careerbuilder.com/share/aboutus/pressreleasesdetail.aspx?sd=4%2F24%2F2014&id=pr819&ed=12%2F31%2F2014. 24 April 2014.

pieces that come in the mail, or the prevailing opinion among their classmates and teachers.

My youngest son was considering two universities during his senior year in 2015. One university would cost $233,500 over the course of four years, and the other $67,500. We found a study that indicated the return on investment over twenty years would be higher at the less expensive university. Even though the estimated starting salary would be higher coming out of the more expensive university, his earnings over twenty years would not be much different, and he would get to keep more of the earnings (rather than put them towards student loans).

With all of my children, the college mail started sophomore year and heated up exponentially in the senior year. University of Chicago was particularly impressive with regards to the quantity and quality of their marketing campaign. But having facts at their fingertips will equip your student with the knowledge to make a good choice from both an educational and financial perspective.

IT STARTS WAY BEFORE HIGH SCHOOL

As parents, we want our kids to be successful. And while the opportunities discussed in this book come to students in high school, the preparation starts long before. Raising the type of student who will work hard for good grades, who will want to get into a great college, and who will want to earn scholarships can only happen if we raise a child who believes they can accomplish hard things, and a child who has been encouraged and supported in developing the skills needed to set and tackle challenging goals.

Here are some suggestions for the parent who wants to raise their child to become a motivated and capable student.

Read, Read, Read – Read to your children when they are young, and encourage them to read when they can. Find books that not only entertain, but that also stretch the imagination and encourage dreaming of achieving hard things.

Play time vs. PLAY TIME! Play with your children. Play the games that stretch the mind; counting games, calculating games, spatial, spelling and language games, etc. In our family, Sorry and Parcheesi were early favorites. Counting to twenty when you earned the right to move that far was a big challenge, but a great skill and confidence builder. As the kids got older Monopoly, with the calculating of how much you owe and how much change, became a great way to develop math skills and math confidence at an early age. Scrabble, Boggle, and later a homegrown version of Scattergories, were great for learning to think about words. Puzzles with pieces and words also stretch the ways the brain will think and develop as well.

Unstructured play has its place in every child's life, but if you make time to regularly be a part of the play activities, you will see great results.

Encourage Verbal Communication
- Technology can often take the place of talking. Your student needs to practice the art of verbal communication, not only as an essential life skill, but also because many college and scholarship applications include an interview.

In your own family, encourage conversation at the dinner table, while driving in the car, and in all your family activities. Consider having a family discussion to establish limits for use of texting and other non-verbal communication techniques.

Look for organizations that offer opportunities for public speaking and social interaction (Boy Scouts, Youth Group, K-Kids, and other service clubs for kids). By encouraging your student to develop and refine their communication skills you will give them a gift that will pay big dividends in educational, relationship and career pursuits.

Help kids choose wisely how they spend their time - When your children are young they should have the chance to be children, with a healthy dose of play time mixed with experiences that teach them the value of hard work and the fulfillment that comes from having responsibility for your own choices.

I propose the following action plan to help children value time and practice choosing to spend their time productively:

1. Make a list of the ways in which you would like your child to spend his discretionary time (exercising, reading good books, practicing a musical instrument, learning to type, doing his chores, writing stories, drawing, painting, creating, etc.)

2. Make a list of the things your child chooses to do with his free time (TV, gaming, surfing, texting, music, reading, sleeping, etc.)

3. Create a list of activities your child can do that will earn him the freedom to choose his free time activities for a certain length of time (perhaps include your child in the formulating of this plan).

30 minutes of this   to earn 30 minutes of:

30 minutes of this	to earn 30 minutes of:
reading	movie or television
piano or guitar practice	online time
bike riding or trampoline	phone time
bedroom or laundry chores	Xbox time
writing or drawing	

For example, if your student wants the privilege of using the computer, television, cell phone, tablet or game consul for 30 minutes, he or she must spend 30 minutes in a mind or body strengthening activity.

And of course it goes without saying that all homework must be done before any free time can be earned.

Some other mind and body strengthening activities for your list might include:

- Practice math (software, workbooks, etc.) math software
- Write a story, a journal entry or a letter to Grandma
- Play a game that requires the use of math or language (Monopoly, Parcheesi, Scrabble, Boggle)
- Do a puzzle
- Practice typing
- Science related kits or projects.

Your list of activities will vary based on the age of the child and the interests of the child. For example, I had a few children who were avid readers. They passed through a phase when they would choose to read over everything else. Reading is great, but too much of anything can be unhealthy. For these children, at certain times in their life, reading moved to the list of things they could earn. At other times, reading was on the list of required tasks. Being flexible, aware and involved with your child will result in a teenager who is equipped with the skills to set challenging goals and diligently work to achieve success.

If you work to raise children who participate in a healthy range of play activities, practice communicating verbally, and take an active part in choosing how to use their time, you will give your children a great gift.

Children who practice the skill of choosing to use their time on activities that require a bit of effort will not be afraid to tackle school projects, test preparation, and scholarship applications as they get older. Another benefit you can expect is that your child will learn to value time as a great asset. And in making the choice, your student will begin to understand their own ability to shape their destination and their destiny.

Made in the USA
San Bernardino, CA
30 January 2016